Anatomy of

Anatomy of a Divorce

Anatomy of a Divorce

poems by

George MacBeth

HUTCHINSON
London Melbourne Auckland Johannesburg

© George MacBeth 1988

This edition first published in 1988 by Hutchinson Ltd,
an imprint of Century Hutchinson Ltd,
Brookmount House, 62–65 Chandos Place, London WC2N 4NW

Century Hutchinson Australia Pty Ltd
PO Box 496, 16–22 Church Street, Hawthorn, Victoria 3122, Australia

Century Hutchinson New Zealand Ltd
PO Box 40-086, Glenfield, Auckland 10, New Zealand

Century Hutchinson South Africa (Pty) Ltd
PO Box 337, Bergvlei, 2012 South Africa

Photoset by Rowland Phototypesetting Ltd
Bury St Edmunds, Suffolk
Printed and bound in Great Britain by
Anchor Brendon Ltd
Tiptree, Essex

British Library Cataloguing in Publication Data
MacBeth, George
  Anatomy of a divorce: poems
  I. Title
  821'.914   PR6063.A13

ISBN 0-09-172684-0

For my son, the survivor

ACKNOWLEDGEMENTS

Some of these poems have appeared in the following magazines: *The London Magazine, The Listener, The Literary Review, The New Luxury, PN Review, The Rialto, The Scotsman, Stand, Strawberry Fare, Words, Writers' Monthly*; some were in the following anthologies and supplements: *New Poetry I*, the *PBS Christmas Supplement 1983*, *Poets For Africa* and *Poems For Poetry 84*; and some were broadcast on Radio Three in 'The Living Poet' and 'Poetry Now'. To all the editors involved my thanks are due.

Contents

Part One

Aconite
Another Look at Rhubarb
A Field of Rape
Remembering the Middle Ages
Dame's Violet
The Pigeon
September Walk
The Sovereign
The Vision of Gustavus Helsham, Esquire
Remembering Mincemeat
Moths at the Window
The Judas Tree

Part Two

A Fairy Story
A Voyage Round the Atlas
Letter to an Intermediary
Easter Monday
Advice From the Extractor
Gripes of a Former Dryad
The Adventure
Night Thoughts
In My Valentine, I Say
The Dream
The Viceroy
The Inquisition
Bad Friday
Pavane For a Succubus
The Vandal
Mirror to the Black Sheep and Back
The Casket

Foreword

The poems in the first section suggest a geographical background, and perhaps offer an ominous trailer, for the poems in the second section which really give the book its title. The divorce is not only – for the purposes of these poems – the quarrel of a man with the woman he loves, but also of a poet with his Muse, and a believer with the power he trusts.

George MacBeth

Part One

Aconite

Preceding even snowdrops, gold on white,
And unobtrusively green-ruffed and slight,
There comes the first, the deadly, aconite.

Why should each year begin with poison laid
Along the gravel, under yews, in shade
Wherever something shelters, grove or blade?

It always does. The laurustinus dies,
The last rose perishes, the daisy flies,
Even the precious hebe shrinks and cries.

Frost comes. Then icy remonstrance of hail
And sleet like pebbles rattled in a pail
And all, and every one, to no avail

Against those thrusting yellow bullet heads
That everything in nature loves and dreads,
The wicked ladies in their shadowy beds.

Aconite! Who has poisoned her, and found
A place to bury her in level ground
Up to her neck, to shiver with no sound,

Her petals closed, her sepals green and wide,
And all of England frosted at her side,
A perfect flower, January's bride?

Another Look at Rhubarb

What flowers did we have in that far garden?
Was there a hydrangea, paper-thin,
Or pink, or mottled, in the terrace bed?
Were there spiraea, as I think there were,
As tall as I was, or a little more,
And were there laurels by the road, white-flecked
And firm? And were there roses with their sharky thorns?

I see a statue, of a wilting girl,
In white and rain-stained marble, in the middle.
And all around, in radiating lines
Visible from the window of a bedroom,
The banks of flowers: the gravel, and the grass.
And, far away, towards the taller trees
That masked the gardens of a big Victorian house,

A hut. Yes, there were flags there in that hut,
Of common yellow, as I called it once,
The hue of pride, woven for the LDV.
This was a war that brought hope's blossoms down
And laid them safe in ordinary pots
For plain civilian men to bed and water,
And women, so bereaved, to feel closed anger at.

I see one such by that bed, stooped and smiling,
And round her snow. And later, shrubs, whose names
I don't remember, or I never knew,
Too keen on cricket, or on aeroplanes,
As I was then, to help with weeds or pruning.
I want to now. I mourn for all those days
The lawn lay wild, unmown through my neglect, or pride.

Only the rhubarb, huge and eaten through
By caterpillars, and its waste of ears
Like elephants with green trunks in the ground,
Only that mushy plant, that made us puddings
With milk or custard in a flowered bowl,
Only that sprawling vegetable brings back
How little, and what wasted, gathering was done.

A Field of Rape

Each year I see one, yellow in the distance,
About the same week, early or mid-April,
A coat of gold, a cloth of burning flame.

No-one has thrown it there, or fashioned it
As mantling for a queen, or heraldry,
Or even as the carpet for a fair.

It seres, like mustard. Like a painter's panel
Arranged in abstract to adorn the green,
Or sombre ochre, of our fenland spring.

I watch it from the train, or from a car,
Idling in neutral, or at fifty-five,
Or hurtling at high speed for Lynn, or London.

A field of rape, I say. I know it is
Only a cattle's crop of brassica
To feed the quiet ruminants in winter.

Yes, but it burns. It takes the eye in fire
And rages on the rolling down, or flat
For acre upon acre, dazzling hue.

I touch it in my dreams. I bend, and wade
Through hock-high meadows of its rustling silk
With scents of byre and honey in my nostrils.

Reaching, I chew. Retching, I vomit up
All the unconscious essence of desire
And hawk, and weep, amidst the tottering calves.

I fall upon my face, on cattle pats.
Deep in my dream the rape is close and hot
And what was beautiful at yellow distance

Here in the stalky stubble, thick with dung,
Amazes now no more than sainfoin cake,
Or troughs of wurzels, or the cast lucerne.

Remembering the Middle Ages

In alabaster, in the church, they lie,
Hands crossed, feet on a dog. Suave Latin words
Erect sunk, broken merlons to the sky
    For the Kerviles, and their kind,
Who haunt this house, the children say, like birds
And rattle through its rooms, anchored and blind.

These were the owners, Gawsells, Helshams, Browns,
Forgotten down the years, remembered now
Only as tillage, tax from foreign towns,
    Or tithes in leaking barns,
Or rent surrendered in some muddy slough
By plodding serfs, or Germans bringing yarns.

Abroad they prospered. Suffered mulch at home
And merged in bloody rain through squelching fens
Where nothing qualified the rigid loam
    Or plugged sour thatch
That left the ordinary poor in dens
And let each hen moult, throttled, on her patch.

Such was the comity. The state of grace
Where manors crumbled in the summer dust
And earl succeeded earl, felled by the mace,
    Reared by the golden snood,
And swept as commonalty into rust
Like sword and dagger, and the hail-fouled food.

This was the best of times, the worst of times,
The same as now, the same as yesterday,
With bishops cringing, and with royal crimes,
    With honour stripped in air
For all to see, and pity peeled away
Like skins of onions, and no heart shown bare.

Dame's Violet

I see it from my window, off-white mauve
Behind a red rose, and a berberis.
Hesperis matronalis. Flowers flaunt names
Too pretty to be quite precise, but this
Motherly evening-star, bride of a day
When half the shocked world wakes up, and I say
Good morning to the butcher's broom, still claims

A hint of friendly leaves, a sacred grove
Where lilies of the valley cap their bells
In crinkled edges, and the thorns play games.
Life isn't always like that. And what spells
The death of Latin and its clues to shape
And shows below the man the grinning ape
Is *Homo sapiens*, and our lethal aims.

The Pigeon

It seemed a sort of fête-day there
    Under the smiting sun
At midday in Trafalgar Square
    Where almost everyone
Was happy with the burnished air
    And what the day had done.

It was the warmest of the year
    And all the world looked well
And every stone shone sharp and clear
    As if beneath a spell
Until this happened, and brought fear.
    One pigeon swerved, and fell.

There were a thousand on their feet
    Like eighteenth century men
With hands under their tailcoats, neat
    And purposeful, and then
This one, that wanted seeds to eat,
    Lurched, and then fell again.

The others walked like slates or pails,
    A moving sea of grey
Where all the water surged with sails
    And females ducked away
Hunted, it seemed, by eager males
    And treated as their prey.

The pigeon that had fallen rose
    And it was female, too
Or so, at least, I must suppose
    To judge from the plump two
Stout pouters anxious to propose
    From whom it hopped and flew.

Was this a comedy? Or more
    A tragedy, like rape?
There seemed some puzzle to explore
    Until I saw the shape
Of what had caused the bird to soar
    And flop like crumpled crêpe.

This pigeon, creature of the straw
    And mistress of the rump,
Had one leg severed at the claw
    And shortened to a stump.
How could she live? Escape? Or draw
    Sustenance from her hump?

I sat in silence in the sun
    And saw the square grow dark
Where everything had focused one
    Small, pitiful, grey mark
And what had earlier begun
    With Noah in the ark

Seemed suddenly to end in tears.
    A cloud came, and then rain.
The pigeon might live on for years
    And Ararat bring grain
But I couldn't staunch my flow of fears
    Like water down a drain.

September Walk

The wind in the September wood
With gusts below frail, drooping yews
Brings assonance, like gates blown wide,
And grates my nerves, and grapples, like bad news.

I go out through the ivy, and,
With elbows warm in nylon sleeves,
Shiver at what lies there behind,
The gargoyle leering through the freckled leaves.

August was sober, hot and fine.
Now autumn starts her broken train
And mist films down in cellophane
To cobweb memory with orbs of pain.

The house lies open to its past
And isolation takes a toll
Where each gale snaps a branch or post
And rips bark off, and flecks the rust with coal.

I cross the lawn and pace the field
Hunched against violence and wind
Where ventures from the past have failed
And future possibilities all thinned.

Nettles rose level to my waist.
Now every ear stands cropped and free.
Friends could lean here and face the west
With eyes too sunburned by the south to see.

Stiff, closing cones presage more rain.
They seem embattled by the ground,
Each close and huddled as a rune
Unriddled by the moles that made this mound.

I hear the scrunch of starlings' wings.
Dark, resolute, unmended air
And acrid embers of old wrongs
Burn in a guilty distance there.

The tang of mulberries, the tree
Hung like a tent with strange grenades,
Assuage the taste of what was true
And falsify the shape of graveyard spades.

A rain begins. In earnest now
Steady and damaging right through
Decaying gutters that seemed new
It brings an old, fouled water, cold and blue.

The Sovereign

Under a willow like a woman's hair
On iron painted white, and wrought as leaves,
I watch the evening sky grown lemon-grey
And count the finials black against its ground,
Their fleurs-de-lys like falcons' folded wings.

Haunted by what I am, by what will come,
I hear a heron creaking at the pond
And feel a silence greater than all things,
Dead as the under-echo of a sound,
And then the whisk of rubbing nylon sleeves.

I rise and walk. Far off, kuwick of owls
Calling to mate, and, closer, crunch of shoes
Offer their answer to this utter calm,
A sense of mouths that open, eyes that stare,
Of intervening beak, or toe, or thumb.

I circle past the trees, and soon return
To lights, and cooking, and the garden chair
I paused upon. The sky tastes thin as whey
And willow leaves in dark feel soft and fond.
I crave my house, where steep coal fires burn.

Everything waits. I sense the weight of some
Enormous burden, like a heart attack
Or energy diffusing into glues.
Indoors, he staggers towards me. Palm to palm,
We meet and greet each other. Then he howls.

The Vision of Gustavus Helsham, Esquire

I

First there was fen: unfit for chariots,
And only offering a hold for eels,
A waste of mud and marsh, willows and reed.

Then came the Romans on their sandalled heels,
Carving their names, cowing the marsh for plots,
And sowed a sour belligerence like weed.

The centuries drained off: a pagan creed
Ran from the bowels, and came out as blots,
Staining land, pocking skin on Saxon seals.

The Norse day dawned: a violence of keels
Along the margins of a drift of need,
A cold, profane blight that still twines and rots.

II

Then down the river deltas of the Ouse
Flowed barges, and the barges bore frail bricks
From Thetford workshops, to proclaim the saints.

The churches rose: along the muddy slicks
Serfs foundered, savaged by a haloed bruise,
And built their towers to mollify complaints.

Magdalen, and St Peter's: leaking shoes
Let walls grow rich with dripping Norman paints
And store up energy, like candlewicks.

The candles burned. In place of that strange fix
The soul called ague, and the green-lipped taints
Known as malaria, stuck fears, like glues.

III

Three churches grew, bells tolled. Now there are four.
The fourth one rose apart, banked by the fens,
Where serfs lugged wood and brick to please their lord.

Not that same lord who summoned them before
To bare St German's, or to Magdalen's
Crooked chancel, where the anointing oil was poured.

He was the lord long crucified for men's
Amazement, and his wounds bled ripe and sore.
The unwounded lord, though, was no less adored.

Scribes put their heads to paper, and to pens,
To plan a chapel for his chrismed whore
Or common wife in law, bought by the sword.

IV

St Mary's rose: cooled by a lancet nave,
Bargained from friars, then ceded to the King,
Wheedled by sly monks from the Kerviles' clasp.

Wrenched by a wind, rocked by a tidal wave,
It cried for buttresses, for brutal rasp
Of steel on stone, the knightly barbering.

Far from the sea, it held the see in grasp,
Craving for pardon from the papal ring
That sent one incumbent to an early grave.

Lords of the manor, let them prink and rave
And style themselves our masters. Hasp by hasp,
The caskets whittle down, gape mouldering.

V

One Kervile soldiered. In the Holy Land
He mailed his heart, and sent it home to brood
Dim in a side aisle, under a dead slab.

I see it now, the shape grown sweet on sand,
Then thrown to England, for a thing shown blued
In brass and honour, like a festering scab.

That far crusader had his way, with lewd
And fascinating dames, and carved his brand,
The Islamic fleur-de-lys, white as a stab.

No doubt. All did. So let his relic stand
For all who horsed momentum to their grab
And wasted Palestine, to lift a snood.

VI

Well were they called the children of the goat
In Normandy, long years before they came
To Wiggenhall, and cut their teeth on time.

Their family held sway on ear of oat
And swing of barley, and in oak-smoked grime
Of every cottage where serfs took their name.

As Capravilles they came: and where their moat
Ran round the manor, it condoned a crime.
The lap of water's touch approved their claim.

Droit de seigneur. Taut seamen of dark slime,
Whose eels ran in and out, they raped by rote,
And starving daughters, fissured, owed them shame.

VII

So to the solace of a shared relief
They leaned upon the fantasy of Rome,
Imperial Rome, the papal, rigid seat.

The years ran by. Prey to the dwindled sheaf
Or the beetle-ridden root, the beast on feet
Alive with cattle-rot, they cursed their loam.

Dense, boggy loam. The earth that gave them grief
And brought at length their everlasting home
Under the sod, their hope of heaven's black heat.

They died in anger. Some, unshriven, to meet
What maker in what massive disbelief
How could they say? Dying, below hell's dome.

VIII

And yet some flush of piety, immured
As in the pelican's plucked, flowering breast
There on the font, suffered, and saw them through.

Vassal and lord, they laid their bones to rest
Each evening by a homestead well secured,
If only by the crown, against the few.

There, from the cot, they watched the sunset hue
In gold on staggering gold, far to the west,
And saw it glorious, and fast ensured.

Dark on that orange, everything seemed true
For a moment, and the lacerated breast
Riven open, breathed in fresh air, and felt cured.

IX

The first house rose, wild, in the tossing wind,
Of wood, perhaps: the next, of brick, and where
The brick was vulnerable, waisted stone.

Rain pitted the towered walls, and seasons thinned
The mortar, but the manor house alone
Of all the dwellings round stood high and square.

Stone helped, and much repairing. Quaintly spare
Tilted the foolscap of each finial's cone
And flimsy chimney, up which boys had shinned.

It was a gay house. Tudor to the bone,
Though earlier built, and as elegantly finned
As any dangling heron of the air.

X

I lose it in the mists. The bungling rain
Lets sheets of easy water blur the glass
Of all those glittering windows, midnight lights.

I see the storm pass, like a sense of strain
Tugging the sinews of the mincing grass.
The courtyard and the cheese writhe, as with mites.

Far to the left, the stables, docked, remain
In cusped, round-windowed order. Catamites
And ostlers, mingling, eared, bow to an ass.

Bottomless weaving! As the choir to mass
Proceed, along the arable, one kite's
Wing veers, and crabs the heraldic weather vane.

XI

Such was the weirdness of those ancient days
When numbers wrought in magic, as with runes,
And what was Gothick made a whole world prance.

After the eighteenth century, balloons
Rose from the turrets to astound, amaze
And mark a consul's coming home to dance.

Years had gone by. Venetian, sallow tunes
Played out on violins, and muted plays,
Voiced a reluctance to believe in chance.

A baronet returned. A time of stays
Created a bereaved deliverance,
And madness made a grey light, like the moon's.

XII

Yes, he was mad, the heir who got the house
Fifty years later, and the land as well,
And saw it burn down to a hunting box.

A shooter from the army, loving grouse,
Not to mince words, a dandy and a swell,
Whose world was a panoply of pox.

An accident of tapers, crowing cocks
And women in their stockings, flames to douse
And breasts to finger, sent his house to hell.

Three hundred years flown like a chime of clocks!
And everything once left that he could sell
Posed as a ruin for the harvest mouse.

XIII

Thus I inherited and had the whole.
I sailed from Ireland to appraise and take
A sort of shooting-waste, pheasants and duck.

Willows were everywhere. A sudden bole
Out of the bog revealed what was at stake:
The future of the past, and my poor luck.

I saw the cows, like Cotman, stand in muck
Under the towers, and I felt the soul
Of what had been before quiver and ache.

I might have shuddered, sensing the black mole
Of blind and groping ownership deep stuck
In mould, that nothing could reveal or break.

XIV

No, but I didn't. I resolved to build
And recreate whatever went before
With alterations, and a richer style.

So I contrived my workmen, hired a guild
Of plasterers and painters for a pile
Of elaborate brick, Tudor in glass and door.

The spirit entered, if it did, and filled
What I invented with a devious bile,
And left some puckered evil to explore.

A ghost, maybe. Or slipping slate, or tile,
Where someone might be accidentally chilled
By the lingering past, like a draught along a floor.

XV

All this, and more, I saw within a dream
Sleeping last night here in the former grounds
Where many lords and vassals worked and died.

I woke at seven, seeming to hear a scream
Echoing down some corridor inside
What I would call my heart: infinite sounds.

If I imagined this, then what would seem
To be my vision is a task. Where mounds
Made by the moles uprear, I must have tried.

The crenellations are like living cream
Along the house where I live now with hounds,
Past which the moving swallows dip and glide.

XVI

The dished gong rings for dinner. Day by day,
Gleaned incarnations of dynastic hours
Call me to table, and to stall and prayer.

The swish of servants' dresses clogs my air.
I draw on energy that lifts and sours,
Then filches glebe farms, and a school, for pay.

Railways may come, and fresh milk cooled by showers
Brought up the winding stairs gleam in the flare
Of gaslight, when the land's grown drained and grey.

I, too, grow grey. Blinking before skulled powers,
I plough back their inheritance to clay.
The four posts of my deathbed grant their share.

Remembering Mincemeat

Day after day the sticky mixture stayed.
The bowls it lay in kept cool on grey marble,
Each with a spoon sucked in, as though a spade.

A wooden spoon. The clay of earthenware.
The mixture pummelled out of dough and spice
And apples by the plough-spoon like a share.

A share of earth. And water from the well.
Then subtle seething in the sough of mincemeat.
And something dark, peculiar, in the smell

As if the candles or the drains gone stale
Fermented, and then left a residue,
A tacky resin bitter as an ale.

This was the body we would eat in sorrow.
I knew each night and went to sleep so knowing.
And woke from dreams, tasting the dark tomorrow.

Moths at the Window

None of them, winged with parchment, pass
Into the glowing room, or still
   Their panting eagerness.
   Mummified, husky souls,
     They press
In a perpetual net of will
Against a void. Chill boundaries of glass

Tease them with light. Heads down in rage
Or doubt, like angels packed with sperm,
   They rise to fertilise
   An ancient, airless world
     Where eyes
Float watching them. But hope grows firm.
Everything dies. Darkness will break their cage.

Waiting in bed, stiff and alone,
I see their passion spend itself
   In anxious rioting
   And loss. Doing the same,
     I fling
All of my own love on a shelf
Of nothing, dazzled. But my moth has flown.

The Judas Tree

Somehow betrayal simmered in the air,
    Took roots, and made a tree
   With round leaves. As I walked out there
Under the turrets, watching, we made three,

You and I and the Judas tree, grown sheer.
    The sun set flaming in the west
   Beyond the church, and night strolled near.
I thought that planting something would be best.

So, wet in wellingtons, I dug a hole
    And opened the dry boats
   The seeds had come in. April's mole
Will feel their sprouting on his velvet coat's

Resilience. You will be back by then,
    Ready for life and spring.
   Italian gold will shrink. This den
Of icy worth will glitter like a ring.

Meanwhile, I trowel earth. A failing sun
    Tips into fenny mire.
   Indoors I light white cubes, and one
By one they blaze to make a bitter fire.

Part Two

A Fairy Story

Once upon a time there was a fairy. And the fairy owned an angora rabbit, who lived in a cage. Every morning the fairy spread his wings, and fed the angora rabbit with honeydew.

Every evening, when the sun went down, the fairy furled his wings, and shook out a ration of primroses, for the rabbit to pasture on.

They seemed a happy couple. The seasons changed, and the snow replaced the fallen chestnuts, through which the fairy walked on tiptoe, and on which the rabbit stared, with hooded eyes.

Then one day, when the sun failed to come out, the rabbit escaped, and was killed by a stoat. And the fairy, who had little experience of grief, cut his wings off, and turned into a toad.

A Voyage Round the Atlas

I sailed along the map of Italy
With you in tow. I took a ship to Crete
And there you were, waiting to be relieved,
Still at your post. I had a mind for Turkey,
For Samarkand, for Mozambique, for Chad.
Owning the means to love, passports for joy.
But you said, no. Let's winter here in Crete
And laid your bright hair down to brush my feet.

So page fourteen was cancelled. I redeemed
A grave deposit on a Bedouin tent
I'd hired beyond Persepolis, at least
An idea of one in a pool of freckling
Where someone upset his coffee. So we paused,
Easing our heads on pillows of deep red,
The British Empire, and in plaits of blue,
The deep blue seas, the oceans of dire dread
Haunted with cherubs, and with hulls of spice
Delineated by the hatching pens

Of ancient scribes. Near to us tribes of nomads
Confounding sheep with their unwieldy turbans,
Hallooed on camels, and were quick to come
Selling us wine. I drank, and you were gone

Under the stitching of the spine, it seemed,
Out of the borders, and beyond the cover,
Into a night where nothing stirred save echoes
Of a multitudinous population of locusts.

I crawled back in – for I had stepped and seen
The *horror vacui* on the brink of shelves –
And shed my tears on Madagascar's hills
Indigo as Portugal. I was alone
I knew then in a muster of conditions
Fertile for work, uneasy for true love.

I took the index for my guide and flew
From word to word, an Arab on a roc,
Spelling the names of wonder, Greece, Cathay,
Paris, Damascus, Montenegro, Rome

Until I came at last to Venezuela.
There, in my tears, I knew that you would creep
Home to your hacienda, where my hand
Settled on gravid mountains, etched in grey,
And rubbed a fragment of an avocado
Someone had spilled one morning from his meal.

Then I lay down and slept, losing the world.

Letter to an Intermediary

Dear Madam, knowing your principal is away
I take the liberty of addressing
You in person. School is a nuisance, I know.

So are thighs, requiring the plucking-out
Of invisible hairs. How is your face mask?
Are the imaginary moles

Between your toes alert in their fortresses?
I have heard
Here, the lowing of innumerable donkeys

Reminding me of Morocco. This was, of course,
In a dream. Are you growing
More skilful, tea time by tea time,

In the video games of a calculated perspective?
Strike that. I am being clever,
Wanting to amaze you with my erudition.

Very little happens. I am sleeping well
When the hot-water bottles are drained
Of Bailey's. I drink their milk to your memory.

Now, in a windy twilight, as I sit
Arousing distaste in the fireflies
To judge from their sighs in the grate,

I recall your disgusting itching, the
Loud velours of your burps. What it is
To be a versifier and switch senses!

Come home soon. Intercede for me
With the Grand Panjandrum on Her return
To seek a fare and an opportunity for travel.

Together, we may still explore
The alps of Magdalen Road, the upper delta
Of the Ouse. I suspect the crocodiles,

In my pleasure, of brushing their foul teeth
On a sandbank already
To yawn for you. But I may be premature.

The year dotes in its margins. A chill
Arrests the pack ice. If Our Lady
Were to understand better the ways of idiocy

There might still be muffins and parasols,
At least for Easter. Let us hope so.
In the meantime, be steady. Row safely

Through the minefields of Bristol.
I hear there are knives in chip shops and irregular
Swains under plane trees. I worry. Be careful.

Easter Monday

Although it is far ahead, I am already
Going to church in my head. That is,
Conducting a proper tour of the Mansion. I
Steer, for instance, through the smells of the hall
Ignoring the dog-shit. I pluck a rustle

Of wintering stems from the neck
Of a carousel, I mean a vase
Dedicated to the emergencies of passion.
This was our Christmas. These were our ceremonies
Prepared for a boy with a bruise

Who might have been up before us, minding stockings
With a cold potato-gun. He might,
But he wasn't. Nor is he now,
Ready as I am for intervention
And renewal, chalking Postman Pat nuances

On a skirting board. I polish alone
As I shall no doubt polish when the day comes,
Minding my own business. That may be yours,
I agree it should be. Noblesse oblige
And the jugs of water tarnish without discrimination

Where the roof came in, and bequeathed
A benison of tears. Yours and mine,
Mouldering on the cross of an apple branch
That will burn with a sweet savour,
Greet (as they say in Scotland) and sequester

Providence. Anyway, let me opine
That the castle will glimmer in its own
Aura, without benefit of candles. The Cherry
Blossom I put on boots will extract
A dominion of glory from leather.

I shall walk as on Afghan carpets,
Manufacturing my own delight in your presence
Even by imagination. Where would the fun be
In a universe too patently inhabited
By the ecstasy of an owner? That one exists

I know by the beating of my heart,
Now that I rise, wanting tea,
And feel the sense of age rested
Under a banyan tree, its rafters of concern.
They are yours, those. They are there always. I feel them.

Advice From the Extractor

Good morning.

Lot to be said for getting it all
Out of your system, eh? Plenty of bile here.
Spit in the bowl.
I'd say you've been bad-mouthing
Some woman – as our American
Cousins put it – through too many poems.
Clean up your act. Lie

Back in the chair and look directly
Into the light. There. Is that
Better? See things
More clearly now, do we? My
Own experience, having
Had, as one might say, the sort of
Unassimilated fillings

We're talking here, is that only
Time, the great healer,
Allows a proper connoisseurship
Of spitefulness. Better wait.
Wash your mouth out. Those
Fragments of bone tissue
Get under the tongue. Later on

You can bitch at will
About their inadequacies, whoever
They are. For the present
I'd go easy. Watch
Your bite. Lay off the excess sugar
As well as corrosives. It won't
Help. You'll

Find you're better off
With a bitter detachment. Use
A good rinse, a
Scouring powder on Sundays. Come back
In a month. We'll
Take another look. Maybe
Compare notes. Get together for a gargle.

Goodbye.

Gripes of a Former Dryad

And what about the walled garden? All those
Funny herbs
Drying themselves out by the bricks. I know
I put them there, but it gives
Me the willies remembering.

Same with the speedwells. Their blue
Eyes watching
Me out of the clover. Cuckoopint
In a portion of wood
Bare of timbre. And what about

The unbased logs meandering
In and out
Of the snowdrops? The aconites,
Their acolytes. Etc. I throw up
In my dreams recalling days hunting

For firewood with the gnomes
Rubbing their hands
In glee behind the hawthorns. One, yes,
I know there was only
One. And what about the nights

Gripping stone with a tendril
Of ivy reaching through
To do a bat-job in your hair?
And what about
The dazed mornings, abasing yourself

Before a jar of milk. Waiting
For a hedgehog
That never came. Sending messages
Over and over
Again to a flycatcher throbbing

Its guts out on a bough. And
What about now, unable
To dig the manure out
Of my hind brain, haunted
By the love affairs of your squirrels and gnats?

The Adventure

Was I set off one day walking
Carrying my heart. I went upstairs first
And there was a wash-hand basin, stinking cold,
Where someone threw it in, scrubbing
With a tough brush
Until it was clean. Well, it was clean

Before, I thought. So I took the back stairs
Down to the kitchen. There by the stove
Another one stood stirring a can of soup
In a saucepan. Fat spitting
Fell on my hands. Look out, he said,
Seizing me by the heart. Then he

Pitched it, all frozen as it was, hard
As a hamburger, into the
Boiling broth. So it sizzled, and softened.
Well, it was soft before. Soft enough,
I thought. But he said, no. No,
You say? Then I was tired. I

Took a turn down the corridor, slank
Through to the hall and up
The front stairs to bed. O, it was good
To lie down to rest my weary heart,
Then – ouch! There were thistles,
Tearing thistles, right out of Scotland's pride,

Burning the sheets. I felt my heart
Shrink at their touch. It bristled
And felt on fire. Well, it was hot
Enough before. A barrel of flame,
So it seemed to me. No, said a man
Standing there by the wardrobe

Setting shirts on a hanger. O, no.
Your heart was a dull old stick,
It needed stimulating. You see
The adventure is that you never know
How dirty and hard
Your heart is, or how ordinary,

Until one tries you. Be assured
You are wanted
When such trouble was gone to here
In your own subtle house
To commit your heart to these trials
Which it has come through so well. It shows

Your importance.

Night Thoughts

Boot Bear, last night
I saw the furry cows with
Long horns. They were in
A dream. I lay watching
Them hour after hour
In my cuddly
Pyjama world. Were you there?

You're not always, are you? I
Sometimes tear the pigs
Off the wall I get so angry
With you not being
There. I did once,
Anyway. I might do again,
If they put them back.

Anyway, I miss you now
In the special blueness. I
Want you here, under
The brown mammoth before
He digs his white tooth
In my eye. He sometimes
Does. You know he does.

I love him more than you. He's
Here, anyway. He only
Cries when I throw him
Out on the floor. You cry
Often. Sometimes you cry
In my mind long after I've
Gone to sleep.

Who else cries? Does the moon
Cry in the lake? Moons
Don't cry. Moons
Have a long way to go before
Morning. I wish I did.
I want to come
On a train and see you.

I want to get up and
Put my sailor suit on
With a scarf and a hat. I
Want to fall asleep
Properly in the train and
Wake up and
You be there.

Boot Bear, you're so sweet. When
Are you coming
To see me? If
I go to sleep straight away
Now will you come
In a dream and say
Good night to me? And kiss me?

Please come.

In My Valentine, I Say

'Heart of my Heart, Rough
Diamond, Most
Clubbable of Persons, to
Call
A spade a spade, I

Miss you more than a Joker
Should. In the two
Suits I brought home from
The cleaners today, I see
The stains

Of so many games we spent
Together, ineradicable.' 'Your tricks
Are well taken, Black
Jack,' you
Reply

With a copy of *Harper's
And Queen*, and a King-
sized
Hamburger in your fist. 'Monday
May be

More remarkable. Let's play
Bézique,
Silly Buggers, Whist, or
Whatever you want
To. Whoever

Dares, wins. I'm in
The red, but I'll bet
You a jockstrap to
A pony you
Don't get AIDS

Before I do.' 'It's a sick
Valentine,' I say,
'When your former partner
Holds no trumps, and can't
Bid except

With a swizzle-stick. I'll
Raise you one, see
You sometime. But the boy
Has a royal flush
Down one side of his patrimony, and the girl

Never left
South America in
Her blue genes. It's a full
House, yes, but
Where are the four aces, the points of the compass?

Tell me that, Wild Card.'

The Dream

I have a dream. You're
Ahead of me, driving
A Volkswagen Convertible.

Who leans out,
In his black Ulster,
Sketching the road?

In the distance,
I see the Sugar Beet Factory
Going down like the Titanic.

I don't stop
At Pete's
For an ice cream and some firelighters.
But you do.

I'm blocked
By the chicken-run and the bridge.

Then we pick up speed.
You tell me
Through a megaphone
That you plan to get married.

At the roundabout
It's the loch at Loch Dhu Lodge.
Who is it fishing with you?

No, it's a dream.
The real loch
Is further on, by the railway station.

You'll drown there,
Somebody calls out
From a postal van, unless you wake up.

Who cares?
You're coming round
The bonnet, holding divorce papers.

The Viceroy

Neither a surfeit
Of panamas, nor a legend
Of cruelty will suffice. I
Instead ache for some simple silence.

Riding this morning (in a taxi) through
The rainy purlieus
I smoked seven Marlboro in a row.

Alliteration gets you nowhere.
I have cut
Out alcohol, instructed
The young lady to vote for cheese and spaghetti.

Post me a sweetener, you say. But how?
Just stop
Going on and on about how many inches
There are in a grudge.

Bad weather
Assembles in crumbs, reminding me always
Of a little villa in the sun, someone
More adequate with a Hoover.

It will happen. When it does,
Expect a remarkable increment
In courtesy, a plague even
Of benefits. Meanwhile,

Go easy (will you?) on wrecking
The telephone with a hatchet.

I do remember.
Mostly in my spleen, but there are days

When our jubilee
Re-creates itself like eight miles of ships
Off Malta.

Believe me,
You burn dimly in your saucer.

But you never go out.

The Inquisition

Where were you last night?
Don't answer. I
Know where you were.

What was his name?
Don't answer. I
Know his name.

No, I don't want to know
Who you weren't with. When
I say you were
With someone, that's where you were.

Pass me the tongs.

You were where
I say you were, weren't you?
That's better.

Why were you there?
I know why, but I
Want to hear you say why.

The jug.
Swallow this.

Now tell me
Why you were where I don't
Want you to go.

Why you go there
With someone you know I don't want you to go with.

No, I don't want to know. I
Want to hear
The sound of my own voice going on and on.

Going on and on and on and on and on.

Tear out her tongue.

That's better.

Bad Friday

After the sponge of vinegar, and the
Ghost being given up, not
Forgetting his three
Teddy Bears, I
Swaggered upstairs to the dressing room, and
Ransacked
Your wardrobe. Ran my hands
Through a load of cold silks
And thought, Nevermore
Quoth the Raven etc, then
Pissed it all away
In a
Bad case of the shakes.

Makes thirteen lines. Exactly.
Can't
Remember what
Happened after
The vomiting. I may
Have emptied the chamber pot
In a vacuum, or sold
A round of tears to Harper's Bizarre, or
Just laid me down
On the goatskin
Rug, and had it off
With my own
Conscience. What else is there to do?

Nothing. No, not then
Or later, so it seems,
Re-running the good news –
We'll see
Each other sometimes – on
The back side
Of my torn belly. Listen. You
Don't die
From the blood
Oozing out, you
Die of suffocation, asthmatic
For tenderness. But don't worry. It gets
Better. When you're ninety-nine

And too senile to remember
They pick you up and breathe
New life in your old
Wheeze-box. Here is
Your son. Take, eat
Some fish fingers with him.
Look. He
Loves you, yes,
He really calls you Uncle Jim
Once in a while. Strike
That. These were the thirty-nine
Articles, but I
Make them fifty-two, a house of cards.

Pavane For a Succubus

Who came yesterday
And has long black hair and
A big mouth and

Who likes a bit of
How's your father. She won't
Be coming

Again unless
I can go uphill inside
The Lazarus tube.

One more time, she
Said, one
More time, and the Leaning Tower

Of Pisa shook
Its money
Into the abattoir.

I remember, I remember
The days
When there was plenty for

Everybody, even
Fat-face, and
Her pimply bum.

Some were in rags, and
Some were in
Gingham, some

Came trembling, and some
Atishooed, and
Some just came

Faster and faster and
Louder and
Louder until it

Was quite
Indecent. Hail,
Pornography,

Solace of lonely men,
Abettor
Of bad verses,

Good mixer, annulling
Nothing, even
The night jackets

Reeking of semen, the
Blood-rotten
Ambulances

Of the will, the
Greek facetiousness
And its analogue,

A discriminating hell-cat
With a long memory. I
Know the score, toss

Me a scrap
Of paper, set
Me going, wax

My nut-case, and
I can get off
Your back.

It's a long haul
To seventy-
Five, and the lights going out all over Europe.

I need her beckoning
Thumbs and her
Bradford sauce.

Lady Pornography, pretty
Girl, my loo chain.

Pull and I come.

The Vandal

The boy
Leans forward, shifting
An avocado, wild
Hair above sailor suit, the
Intent
Absence, masquerading as a balance of
White and blue to the left.

Red, where
Is red, except
On the wall behind the black
Sycamore of brocade where the master
Lifts
His D'Annunzio fingers, intoning
To his own soul.

Behind
And against the dying
Sun, blue as blue, the inflaming
Subjective, crazy
Eyes of their daughter, smashing
Out of the frame, into the
Gaze of the painter.

You
Are there, the pin
In the middle, blue
Too, these are the days of blue,
Your dead centre
Triangle welding still the
Explosive quincunx.

And
You are smiling, calm
As a message, that
No-one wants to know, about
How the clock halted
Near to twelve is announcing the
Dawn of something.

Sometimes
I would like to ram a knife right
Through that smile, making
The sign of the cross, with
The sideways and upwards thrust
Of a Japanese, committing
Suicide.

Let
It rest, along
The wall I pass every day
To the room
Where the cat sleeps in the grate, and
A holdall of anguish bursts
Into flame.

Mirror to the Black Sheep and Back

I used to see him
Crouching
Down with his face in your
Fur, hoping
No-one was watching.
                        Perhaps
He was thinking about your unskinned
Friends
Learning to walk on the windy hills, the
Sun
Burning their black faces, and you
Here
Headless outside a drawing room
For people
To wipe their feet on.

He kissed your fur. He
Loved you,
Surrogate as you are, helping
Him through. Do
You remember? It
Was a long
Time ago, I forget his name. But here,
Under my scratched silver,
I keep a souvenir
Of his unshaven face, streaming with tears.

Yes, I remember
The rough
Touch of his chin, the flat
Scrunch of his groping hands. He was
Like a
Bare foot in the middle of the night
Or someone tripping. It

Meant very little, but then
To me here
Day after day sleeping the sleep
Of the damned, not much does. But

Thank you for reminding me. He
Must have been nice. It is
Nice when someone tries

To cut through the plush of convention.

Good morning, warden.

The Casket

'Then Language, turning at the door,
Sent back one phrase, I love you,
To stay behind.

The Rolls was running, the chauffeur
Slapped his gloves at the wheel.

Sun glistened. A dazzling experience
Writing plays, being a screen writer's
Dream, awaited Language.
                            She nuzzled in furs,
Shifting her one jewel on a lean finger.

Then she handed it back. I love you,
Shines like a fragment of emerald
Now in my casket.
                  Outside
A storm nags, deep snow piles on the grating
Above the coal hole, the crows are asleep
In a wild cradle of difficulties.

Let Language go. Racing the moon
Across Europe to the valid, fresh capitals
Where men with canes are painting.
                              I am happy
With only three words to my name
In a little house echoing with reminiscence.

I bask in the glow
Surreptitious out of the sly velvet, the
Purples of enclosure where I have laid
My one jewel, a security against madness
And all the deaf energy of unrelenting time.

Be lucky, Language. Grow rich
In your own scenario, pocket millions.

One lurks here who remembers you.'

Thus dreamed
The carver of dumbbells, gilding
A pantoum by candlelight in his attic,
At a loss for words.